The Colour War

The Colour War

Poems by

W. Luther Jett

© 2024 W. Luther Jett. All rights reserved.
This material may not be reproduced in any form, published,
reprinted, recorded, performed, broadcast,
rewritten, or redistributed without
the explicit permission of W. Luther Jett.
All such actions are strictly prohibited by law.

Cover design by Shay Culligan
Cover image by Steve Johnson on Pexels
Author photo by Steve Harvey

ISBN: 978-1-63980-672-0

Kelsay Books
502 South 1040 East, A-119
American Fork, Utah 84003
Kelsaybooks.com

*I still believe, in spite of everything,
that people are truly good at heart.*

—Anne Frank
July 15th, 1944

Acknowledgments

The author wishes to express gratitude to the following publications:

Beltway Poetry Quarterly: "The Colour War," "Poem Written While Standing in Prayer," "Prayer"
Bourgeon (Mid-Atlantic Review): "How Many Fingers?"
Live Encounters: "Wartime Lullaby," "Anthem for Everywhere"
Migrations and Home: The Nature of Place (anthology, NatureCulture LLC): "Landays"
New Verse News: "Fairy Tales," "Crossing the Dnieper," "Lines Written in a Subway Car"
Support Ukraine (anthology, Moonstone Press): "Whoever You Are"

The author is indebted to many people who have offered feedback on these poems—particular thanks are due to Yvette Neisser for her editorial suggestions as this book went to press.

Contents

There

The Colour War	15
Late February 2022	16
Nuclear Clock	17
March Lions	18
Fairy Tales	19
Whoever You Are	20
Beasts	21
Stains That Don't Fade	22
Between the Borders	23
Journey	24
Crossing the Dnieper	25
A Small Crack	26

Somewhere

Quantum	29
News in Brief	30
The Field	31
The Cutty Wren	32
Lines Written in a Subway Car	33
How Many Fingers?	34
Orchestra	35
Arson	37
The Keen Edge	38

Everywhere

Anthem for Everywhere	41
Picture of the Year	42

Landays	43
One Drop	44
The Day When We Say "Enough!"	45
Heritage	46
A Wartime Lullaby	47
Motherland	48
After	49
Prayer	50

There

The Colour War

He wants an end to colour—sky
only tarnished silver—land
a sickly pale of mud churned
by endless trucks, trucks
that come in the night
with plenty of warning, but still
unbidden. A world of grey
that cannot stand. Our arsenal
must be a prism. We shall lay
new sod—green, lush—
where the land is scarred. We
shall break open the coffers
of colour and paint the sky again,
blue and gold. Let us go now,
down to the riverside. Let us gather
round, smooth stones, pile them
on the shore. He forgets
that grey is also a colour.

Late February 2022

On February 24th, 2022, Russia invaded Ukraine in a major escalation of the Russo-Ukrainian War, which began in 2014.

I am watching this world.
I am watching dark choppers
swoop over a city. Ice sheaths
the branches here. I am watching
thick clouds of smoke. Soot soils
red tile. Families huddle underground.
A string of border guards by the sea
screams defiance at a battleship.

Elsewhere, a thousand city squares
throng with the indignant.
Monuments lit with colours
scorn those who fear our rainbows.
And it is not enough. It is not
all that can be done and yet,
and yet it is something. Those guards
were atomized by exploding shells.

There is no good way to die.
But there are worse
ways to live. The ice breaks
from the trees in tiny shards
that bounce as they strike
yellow ground. I am watching
the sun break through. Because
the sun must break through.

Nuclear Clock

February 28th, 2022

Just before midnight
my bed begins
to shake. Tremors
roil the earth beneath
my home, wave
after wave. Now
a strange wind passes
through the walls.
I try to raise
my arm. The wind
holds it in place.
I open my eyes. Light,
that has no business
burning fills the room.

March Lions

In almost-spring crocuses
emerge, yellow and blue.
First brave blossoms dress
young trees. A man reads
at a table in the park.
A gust of wind tears off
my hat, as if to say:
"Salute!" Girl on swing
pumps higher and higher.
While in a city far away
they fill old bottles
with petrol, stuff the necks
with strips of torn sheets.

Fairy Tales

for Bucha, Ukraine, April 2022

Let's pretend the moon
is made from cheese, and bees
go there when they die,
and the river runs backward
on alternate weeks, and, oh,
the tallest peaks
are covered in ice cream—
you could climb them in just
ten giant steps—or fly.
Yes, let's pretend that we
can fly. Also, let's pretend
that summer will have no end.
The rifle isn't loaded. Those
are not dead bodies there,
bloating in the city square.

Whoever You Are

Face etched by hazard
on this grim street
which leads to a broken
bridge—you carry
nothing but your papers tied
with string, a drained phone,
worn blanket draped
over shoulders curled,
cold—one hour ago
planes strafed your flats—
no, not planes, but the men
who pilot them—held you
in their sights one brief
moment before they veered
south to burn the hospital,
so you, you escaped
for anywhere else—Now
will tell your story? I can't
shake this—Whoever
you are—I love you.

Beasts

Sometimes we forget
our eyes are open
and the night gets in.
Then it is no longer
safe to walk the garden.
There are beasts.
When you meet a beast
on the path at night,
call it by its proper
name. Speak firmly,
but don't cry out.
The beast can sense
shrillness. Bring up
your words from your
diaphragm as opera
singers are trained.
Take control
of darkness this way.
The beast cannot
own you nor place
copper pennies
over your eyes.

Stains That Don't Fade

Sky no longer
blue spreads—
stains pale cotton
dark—spilt wine,
ink, blood—
repeated pattern,
ancient lie.

Crumbled wall
below blue meadow—
torn skirt, faded
muslin, strand
of steelwire shines—
new wound.

Between the Borders

You wander deep
through amber fields—
finger a shred
of fabric caught
in fence-wire,
wonder
whose flag flew
here—those
burnt days beneath
a waxen sun. Who
ran toward cover,
fell just shy?

Dry grass keeps
well her secrets,
and all round
flowers nod, gone
to seed. Winter.

Journey

Abandon everything—
all those beautiful
pictures and the heirloom vase,
the testimonials, the trophies.
None of that will be
any use on the road,
bomb-cratered and narrow,
where we limp, weary,
wrapped in wool blankets.
The mountain crest carries
a crust of snow, stale bread
our evening meal.
The compass spins wild
as a peregrine's gyre.
There are stones strewn where
once a village bloomed. Air
so thin, here in the high pass.
In spite of all we leave
consumed, below
the valley is green. Smoke
rises and the wind scatters it.
In the end, even the gutter
channels water to the sea.

Crossing the Dnieper

for Tetiana Svitlova, 75, who was shot by a sniper while crossing the Dnieper from Russian-occupied territory to liberated Kherson, early December, 2022.

There is snow on the boat now
where the woman fell
while crossing the river two hours
ago—where the woman
in that moment reached out for
her husband—two
hours ago mid-river the woman
fell—snow covers
the boat—the place where she fell
crossing the grey river—
she was shot—have we mentioned?—
she was shot—that is why
she fell—crossing the river now is
dangerous—there is snow
now to cover the place she—the woman—
bled out crossing
the river—on her way to Kherson

A Small Crack

We scream
into the darkness
in order to fully
recognize the light
when it
sings back

Somewhere

Quantum

Wall—no matter how thick—
how distant the sea—you still
shake when waves pound shore.

Mouth—your silence cannot stop
birdsong as dawn breaks.

Earth utters fire—A world away
sky turns red as fresh blood.

News in Brief

That news you find
in yesterday's cold newsprint
is someone's heartbreak. Dry
words recount elections won
and lost, resignations, plebiscites—
stand-in for dry bones,
the jumble of them by choked
rivers, or strewn across sere plains.
An army passed through
this grey valley. Now, only wind.
But somewhere, a lover
clutches a scrap of red silk
and kneels beneath a tree
whose fruit has shriveled.

The Field

A field of flowers—poppies,
asters, goldenrod—sparkled
in the morning. And though
I knew the price of that field,
still, I loved it and walked
through it—so many colours
surrounded me—blue, ivory,
and deep, deep violet. There
were stones, sharp. And here—
a broken branch. These only
made the field seem more
beautiful. Until one day,
it was noon, the mowers
came and behind them
the harrows. Now all that's
left is raw, red earth—
a wound stretches from where
I stand to a horizon I can
no longer stand to see.

The Cutty Wren

"O where are you going?" said Milder to Maulder
"O we may not tell you," said Festle to Fose...
—13th century English folk song

Place that was a city—
stone on stone, not piled
but thrown—This home
vacated, levelled. All roads out
churned into mud. Steel
has splintered wood.

Smoke veils the horizon.

What was done here
will be done again
and again. Only the cull
of the cutty wren can stop it.

Lines Written in a Subway Car

To the world:

If you can watch this
and have nothing to say
at least have pity.

If you can watch this
and have no pity,
or have pity for one
and not for the other—
It is you I must pity.

And if you will not watch—
for you I have nothing,
nothing to say.

How Many Fingers?

*"And if the party says that it is not four but five—
then how many?"*
—George Orwell, 1984

They would close the stars
in boxes, nail them shut.
Let no-one see what was
nor what might be.

Time will come when you
will pay to paint your own
coffin—pay with a smile.

Tug down the windowshade.
Stuff rags around your doorsill.

Don't mind the din—
the hammer and throb.
It's nothing, and that smell?
Why it's not gas, only
old flowers. Yes, they're wilted.

A drop or two of ether
should revive them.

Orchestra

On this street covered
with dust, jackboot angels
wear uniforms, wield
burning canisters
of mace, of zyklon, of
forbidden knowledge.

They have come
to conduct inspections—
They are the conductors.
The angels point left
and violins go silent.
The angels point right
and drums are muffled.

Electricity cracks open
our sky—a great wind
raises the dust in
columns. Angels ask
to see your papers, your
teeth, the snapshots
in your smartphone.
This is not a request,
though it will be
phrased as one.

You will be given
a new name—a name
the angels will choose
for you, as there is no
time for orchestras now.
The angels are the only
instruments of the new
order. You are not
even a violin string,
but you will be stretched
until you snap.

Arson

The world is on fire and we,
we are sad. Honeybees
circulate among wild
bergamot, bush clover, lupine.
Red-shouldered hawks keen
through a sky so vivid, blue.
You would not know
that we are burning, but yes,
at night city streets erupt
with gunfire. Children
play in the rubble of bombed-out
buildings—they have no words for
what they have seen. A polar bear
floats on an ice-flow adrift
in a rising sea. Yellow daisies
bloom above the timberline
where once the glaciers slept.

The Keen Edge

In dark morning hours
what is whispered
to the restless wren:
    "Patience"

Already a pale fringe
brushes eastern sky—
Already knife-waves slice
    pale shores.

There is no stillness
which will not shift—
Silence but a frail
    watchword.

Neither thrush nor sparrow
can hold back song—
Patience has become
    complicity.

This day, this day, this day
breaks with fury against
the long, grey jetties—
    Night's throat, slit.

Everywhere

Anthem for Everywhere

Woman. Life. Freedom.

Because so many people
were moving it was easy
to be overlooked. Voices
claimed the streets, then faded.
Tread of a thousand boots,
next, screams—next
cries, next a song.

From deep in the belly—words.
Body overhead suspended.
Uplifted eyes narrow,
stomach clenches—and then
the song. The song they would
ban that cannot be erased, cannot
be unheard. The street
is not theirs—it is ours. That sky—
ours. The song is ours. Our lives
belong to us. They cannot take
what we refuse to give.

Picture of the Year

broken flag brooch embedded
in ice—river of slow fire
and lakes gone dry

Silent hospital room—
chained gate—narrow
passage beneath unseen stars

images of our days

cargo plane packed
full with dreamers—
everyone looks forward

street-dancers—neon city
lit anew—open fields
where children run

where will we go
if we cannot go there?

Landays

for the women of Afghanistan, August 2021

Show me a nation without hope
and I will show you a land without poets.

Even the smallest flower
can cause a desert to bloom.

Two sounds shake the earth—
Guns of war. Trill of one lone sparrow.

Don't weave a shroud of your tears.
Spin them into a ladder.

Long after dust covers everything
water will still find the sea.

One Drop

to the memory of Ukrainian author, Victoria Amelina (1986–2023) who was killed by a Russian missile strike on a crowded restaurant in the city of Kramatorsk, Ukraine.

In a sea of tears—
what is one more drop?
What difference if it fell
from eyes of one who
has seen enough—
who has tried to hold back
for too long? When the rains
saturate the earth, rivers
overflow their banks.
A reservoir will only stand
so much pressure without
release. Then one drop
is all it takes for the dam
to crumble—One drop.
And the same applies
to a sea of blood.

The Day When We Say "Enough!"

A day will come when everyone says
"Basta! No mas! Enough of all this!"
Enough of these little quarrels
we build into mountains of spite,
mountains that erupt to fling fire
and steaming mud at the stars.

Enough of running down narrow
streets as if we were all bulls
chasing imagined cows, or real
cows who want nothing more
than to graze in high meadows.

Why shouldn't we garland ourselves
with crimson and azure flowers?

Enough with all the fences and walls,
the sentry gates, the metal-detectors.
Enough with your swords and your
ploughshares, too—Enough with kings
and men who want to be made kings.

Enough with anyone who pretends
they do not stand naked
on the precipice of understanding
that we are ghosts who seek company
of other ghosts, only so we may sing
together, because the song is all
we ever really needed.

Heritage

My ancestors made war upon each other
at various times and in various
places—from the fields
of Culloden to the Valley
of the Shenandoah,
on the beach at Hastings,
in one hundred nameless villages.

I don't know how far back
it goes—the envy and desire,
the gut-burn of thwarted pride, ache
of hunger, raw pang of fear—
Maybe the trail stretches across
continents, deserts, thick forests,
ravenous oceans. I only know this,
that all their blood, once opposed,
mingles in me. At the last,
it's neither the battle nor the war
but the peace which comes after
that makes this world spin on and on.

A Wartime Lullaby

Kyiv 2022

In the night station, great blue whales
whistle down the long, worn benches.
Their songs are crimson, their breath
smells of oranges. Sleepy mothers wrap
little babies in bunting, sigh and yearn
for a place in the deep country where
the moon is always full. Once the last
train leaves there will be no-one left
to remember the words the whales
whispered, but the babes who doze
in their mothers' long arms will never
stop singing about those whales—
the great hulk of their bodies as they
float through the waiting room,
the way their fins gently wave
in the cool, clean air of that night.

Motherland

Unwind the clock—the secret
spring at last gone dry—our
singer has lost her voice.
Place her on a blanket, bear
her up on wings
to that bright tower where the sea's
song may yet be heard nights
when the stars renew
their vows to the pale moon.

She is not lost—she's only
silenced without sanctuary.
You will be a hand
and strew the grass with petals
where she once walked.
The moon will be our witness.
If there are enough of us
the stars will shout—
Earth will break open and waters
gush forth anew.

After

That awkward morning
>after the dam burst
>after the building collapsed
>after the fire, after the smoke,
>after the vows were taken,
>after the vows were broken,
>after the pleading and the vain
>>attempt at bargaining,
>
>after the show shut down,
>after the bar was raided,
>after the stars fell on Alabama,
>>and on Georgia, and Saskatchewan,
>
>after all that and all that was

was not, after all,
what we were looking for—
>the sun was a blister low in a red sky,
>a certain stillness filled the room,
>you could have heard a fly drop,
>a chill seeped through the crack
>between the window and the sill,

and this was just before that foolish thing
with feathers perched and that dead branch
shuddered with the weight, when released
dew-drops sparkled in relentless light.

Prayer

Say the mud will dry out.
Say the road will clear.
Say the clouds will part.
Say the sea will answer
    the moon's wild call.
Say that when there are clouds
    they will only bring enough rain
    and not too much.
Say that the cardinal perched
    on the dry bush is the same
    cardinal that perched there last year.
Say the road turns but never ends.
Say the land moves but the sea,
    the sea goes everywhere.
Say the sea will never leave us.
Say when you stand on the beach
    at sunset you will think of me.
Say that one sea's sunset
    is another sea's dawn.
Say the winter will have an end.
Say the birds will return north.
Say there will be flowers then.

About the Author

W. Luther Jett is a native of Montgomery County, Maryland and a retired special educator. His poetry has been published in numerous journals, including *The GW Review, Another Chicago Magazine, Beltway Poetry Quarterly, Bourgeon, New Verse News, Potomac Review, Little Patuxent Review, Third Wednesday, Live Encounters, Tuck Magazine, Algebra of Owls,* and *Main Street Rag*. His poems have also appeared in several anthologies, including *Proud to Be* (Southeast Missouri State University Press, 2013), *Written in Arlington* (Paycock Press, 2020), *The Great World of Days* (Day Eight, 2021), and *101 Jewish Poems for the Third Millennium* (Ashland Poetry Press, 2021).

He is the author of five poetry chapbooks: *Not Quite: Poems Written in Search of My Father* (Finishing Line Press, 2015), *Our Situation* (Prolific Press, 2018), *Everyone Disappears* (Finishing Line Press, 2020), *Little Wars* (Kelsay Books, 2021), and *Watchman, What of the Night?* (CW Books, 2022). His full-length collection *Flying to America* was released by Broadstone Books in 2024.

Luther's poem "Holding" received an honorable mention in 2015 from Delaware Literary Connections. In 2001, Luther's poem "Girls in Blue Dresses" placed first in a contest sponsored by Argonne House Press/Wordwrights Magazine. He was also a first-place winner in the 2010 Jean Stainback Schmidt Memorial Poetry contest for his poem "The Chalk House." His poem "Love Song for a Dismembered Country" was selected as a finalist in the Third Wednesday Poetry Contest in 2018. Luther was a winner in the Moving Words Poetry competition sponsored by the city of Arlington, VA in 2011 and again in 2021. His poem "Zeta" was named a co-winner in the 2022 *American Writers Review* competition, sponsored by San Fedele Press. Most recently, Luther's poem "How Many Fingers," published in *Bourgeon,* was nominated for the 2022 Pushcart Prize.

Luther is the facilitator of a monthly virtual open mike sponsored by the Hyattstown Mill Arts Project in Hyattstown, Maryland. He also coordinates two monthly on-line poetry critique workshops.

www.ingramcontent.com/pod-product-compliance
Lightning Source LLC
Chambersburg PA
CBHW070942160426
43193CB00011B/1783